Oskar Schindler

The True Story of Schindler's List

Anna Revell

Copyright © 2017.

All rights reserved. No part of this publication may be reproduced, distributed, or transmitted in any form or by any means, including photocopying, recording, or other electronic or mechanical methods, without the prior written permission of the publisher, except in the case of brief quotations embodied in critical reviews and certain other noncommercial uses permitted by copyright law.

This book is intended for informational and entertainment purposes only. The publisher limits all liability arising from this work to the fullest extent of the law.

Table of Contents

The Early Years

A Spy

World War II

The Hero

After the War

Why

Schindler's List

The Suitcase

Emilie Schindler's Last Days

Lessons From Oskar Schindler

Anti-Semitism Today

The Early Years

Born in Czechoslovakia on April 28th, 1908 Oskar Schindler grew to become best friends with his closest neighbors, two sons of a Jewish Rabbi.

His parents were known as one of the richest couples in Zwittau, Czechoslovakia, where he grew up until the depression in the 30's when they went bankrupt. His father owned a factory while his mother stayed home and took care of Oskar and his little sister Elfriede.

Oskar Schindler was quite popular as a child, however, as a student, there was nothing exceptional about him.

Beginning in the 20's Oskar began working for his father. His job was to sell farm equipment, however, when he married Emilie, it caused problems between Hans and his son so Oskar, began working at a Moravian electric company as the sales manager.

It was during this same time that Adolf Hitler and the Nazi Party started to rise. Hitler told the Sudeten Germans that their ties were to Germany, not to Czechoslovakia and in just a few years, many of the Czechoslovakia Germans joined the Nazi-Sudeten Party.

Oskar Schindler was one of the Sudeten Germans that joined. He did not join the party because he loved the Nazi party, nor because he believed in any of their propaganda, but instead, he joined because he felt that it made good business sense.

Oskar and Emilie were married on March 6, 1928, after dating for only six weeks. The couple lived with Oskar's parents, his father was a raging alcoholic by that time and his mother an invalid.

If Emilie had not fallen in love with and married Oskar Schindler, it is very likely that she would have lived an uneventful average life. She grew up in the Austro-Hungarian Empire.

Emilie's father was a farmer, she had one older brother and was best friends with a Jewish girl while she attended school.

After the two were married, Oskar spent a lot of time traveling due to his business. Because he was a very attractive man who had a ravenous sexual appetite, he quickly became involved with several different women.

It is alleged that one of those affairs, with Aurelie Schlegel, produced Oskar's daughter Emily as well as his son Oskar Jr. However, Oskar denied that the children were his.

Although he lived the majority of his life in debt, he was an opportunist and a very extraordinary man.

After Schindler worked at the Moravian electric company, he served 18 months in the Czech Army becoming Lance-Corporal. Afterward, he returned to the Moravian electric company, however, the company soon went bankrupt.

Afterward, he worked at the Jarslave Simek Bank of Prague until 1938.

During the years of 1921 and 1931, Schindler was arrested repeatedly for public drunkenness.

Before Emilie died, she had stated many times that Oskar Schindler was a womanizer and an alcoholic.

He was cynical, a gambler, a member of the Nazi party, a playboy, and a man that was willing to risk his life and his fortune to save the lives of his Jews.

A Spy

In 1935 Oskar joined the Sudeten German Party and even though he was not a citizen of Germany, but of Czechoslovakia, in 1936, he became a spy for Abwehr which was the Nazi Germany intelligence service.

Later Schindler would tell the police that he became a spy because he had no money, he was deeply in debt and had a severe drinking problem by this point in his life.

Part of his job as a spy was to collect information as well as to recruit more spies. Oskar as to obtain information from railways, troop movements, and military installations located in Czechoslovakia.

On the 18th of July in 1938 Oskar Schindler was captured by the Czech government and charged with espionage. He was imprisoned immediately, however, was quickly released on October 1st due to the Munich Agreement.

Exactly one month after being released, on November 1st, Oskar applied to become a member of the Nazi Party. It was one year before he was accepted.

During that year, Oskar returned to his wife in Zwittau however, as soon as he was promoted to second in command, he relocated Emilie to Ostrava which is located on the Czech-Polish border.

World War II

Oskar arrived in Krakow for the first time in October of 1939. He lived there in an apartment for the next month, however, Emilie continued to stay in Ostrava, visiting Oskar once a week at the very least.

By November of that year, Oskar had Mila Pfefferberg contracted to decorate his apartment. Poldek Pfefferberg, Mila's son quickly became one of Schindler's black-market trading contacts. Eventually, the two would become friends and build a friendship that would last until Schindler's death.

It was also in November of 1939 when Oskar Schindler met Itzhak Stern. It was Josef Aue, the man who had taken control of Itzhak's previous place of employment that introduced the two men.

During this time, it was quite common for the Germans to seize any property that belonged to the Polish Jews. This could be their home, their business or even their personal possessions.

This began as soon as the invasion began, every Jewish citizen was stripped of any rights that they had.

Stern confided later on in life that he was very suspicious of Oskar Schindler for a very long time. Stern's mother had been killed in Auschwitz early on and he was quite bitter.

However, Schindler requested that Stern look at a balance sheet of a company called Rekord Ltd, which he was thinking about purchasing. The company was an enamelware factory that had gone bankrupt just a year prior.

Stern informed Schindler that he should purchase the company instead of running it as a trusteeship under the Main Trustee Office for the East.

Stern explained to Schindler that this would allow him to have more freedom from the Nazis as well as the freedom to hire Jews. Jewish labor at the time was cheaper than Polish labor, and Schindler would be able to use the Jews as slave labor.

He had no problem convincing Schindler of the advantages of hiring Jews. He did as Stern had suggested.

Even though Stern was a Jew and Schindler was a German, the two men had a lot in common. Stern was like Schindler in that he was an opportunist. Many believe without him, there would have been no list. Schindler's Jews would not exist.

It was Itzhak Stern that began giving jobs to Jews who were determined 'non-essential' and were the most likely to be killed. It was Stern who forged the documents for intellectuals to look as if they were experienced factory workers.

The two men's relationship started off purely a business relationship, but by the end of the war, no one could deny that the two were true friends.

Oddly enough, after the war, Stern found out that Josef Aue, the man who had introduced him to Oskar Schindler was, in fact, a Jew himself. Josef's father had been killed in 1942 in Auschwitz.

It was during Oskar and Stern's second meeting that Oskar suddenly blurted out that he heard there was going to be a raid the following day on the remaining Jewish property. This allowed Stern to warn many people and save many lives.

Stern knew at this point that Oskar was trying to gain his confidence, however he was still unsure why.

However, in the winter of 1939, Oskar opened his enamelware factory and was able to bring Itzhak Stern on as his accountant. It was that action, that would change the course of history.

When production started, Schindler was known as shrewd and tireless. He had all of the cheap slave labor any industrialist would want and in only two years, he grew his workforce from 300 to 800.

The Jewish workers that he hired had come from the Krakow Ghetto. For those Jews, it was an incredible advantage. They were able to leave the ghetto during the day and spend their time working in a German factory.

During the early days of the factory, Schindler did not have much contact with his workers, except for a select few such as Stern. However, when Schindler's workers were compared with those of neighboring factories, or those that were stuck in the ghetto, it was Schindler's Jewish workers that seemed to appreciate their jobs the most.

They were able to recognize that it was their Herr Direktor that was protecting them, so much to the point that the Jews began to feel secure in the factory. They even went as far as asking if they could bring their friends and family to work with them.

It took no time for word to get around in Krakow that Schindler's factory was a safe place for Jews to work. One thing that the Jews did not know that Schindler was doing was falsifying their records. Many of the older Jews were reported as being 20 years younger than what they were, the children they, were recorded as adults.

Stern had changed the records of doctors, engineers, and lawyers all so that they would be recognized as skilled metal workers, draughtsmen, and mechanics. It was this that ensured that these people were now essential. The number of lives that were saved due to the records is innumerable.

Itzhak however, knew that all of Schindler's Jews were sitting on the edge of a volcano. It was Itzhak that could see into Schindler's office through the glass door. He remembered that each day, from the morning time until the evening time, visitors and officials visited Schindler. Those visits made Stern very nervous.

He recalled that Schindler would pour vodka for the visitors, and that he would joke with them, but after they would leave, he would be called into Schindler's office. Schindler would close the door and tell Stern why the visitors had been there.

Schindler would tell the officials that he knew how to get the Jews to work, that he wanted more, which was how he was able to reunite so many families.

He never offered any explanation of his actions to Stern, however, Stern began to gradually trust Schindler.

Schindler soon began developing personal relationships with each of his workers. One of those workers was Stern's brother, Dr. Nathan Stern as well as Magister Label Salpeter and Samuel Wulkan who were members of the Polish Zionist Movement. With Itzhak, these men served as Schindler's link to the underground movement.

While family and friends of the workers were being taken to Auschwitz for extermination, being shot in the streets or dying of one of the many diseases that they suffered from in the ghettos, life continued on in Schindler's factory.

In fact, it continued like this until 1943 when all of the Jewish workforce was moved to Plaszow, a labor camp that was located outside of the city.

Amon Goeth was the SS Commandant of Plaszow. The Commandant, passed his time standing on the balcony of his villa with a high-powered rifle which had a scope.

As the children would play in the camp, he would shoot at them. One of Schindler's Jews was only 14 years old at the time, remembered Amon Goeth as vicious and sadistic, another, Poldek Pfefferberg, stated that when you saw Amon Goeth, you saw death.

Stories have been told about Goeth's dogs, which he would sick on prisoners, allowing them to eat the prisoners alive, then only when they had just one last breath in them, he would shoot the prisoners in the head.

The horrors that took place in Plaszow, shocked even those that had lived through Krakow. The workforce that was kept at Plaszow suffered horribly, dying in the camp or being shipped off to Auschwitz in an attempt to complete the extermination of the Jews.

All of Schindler's workers, including Stern had been moved from the ghetto to Plaszow as well as about 25,000 other prisoners who worked in the camps, as well as outside in factories. Stern fell ill one day and sent word to Oskar, pleading that he help. Oskar quickly came and brought Stern the medicine that he needed and continued visiting the camp until Stern was healthy again.

The things that Schindler had witnessed when he visited Plaszow disturbed him greatly and he was also disturbed by the way this camp had affected his factory.

Schindler was becoming helpless by those that were set on destroying the Jewish people. He was no longer able to joke with any of the German officials that came to do the inspections of the factory and it was becoming much harder for him to play the double game.

One event that occurred was when three German officers walked out on the factory floor. They were arguing with each other, one said that the Jew was lower than even an animal. Suddenly he pulled his pistol out and ordered the Jewish worker that was closest to him to eat it as he picked up a pile of filth left on the floor.

The man, shivering did as he was told, choking down the dirt. The officer, made his point, stating that even an animal would not have eaten the dirt.

On another occasion, during an inspection, Lamus, an old Jew caught the attention of the officers. He was quite depressed and dragging himself across the factory. The leader of the officers asked why the man was sad. He was told that Lamus had just lost his wife and his child during the evacuation of Krakow.

One of the officers was told to shoot Lamus so that he could be in heaven with his wife and child. Schindler was left standing next to Lamus when the officer who was ordered to shoot Lamus walked up.

Lamus was told to pull his pants down around his ankles and to begin walking. The old man did just as he was told, confused as to what was going on.

Schindler told the officer that he was interfering with the discipline in the factory. The officer only sneered at him.

Again, Schindler tried, telling the officer that the moral of the workers, was going to suffer and that production would be affected.

The officer pulled out his gun. Schindler almost screaming and no longer thinking about what he was saying offered the officer a bottle of schnapps if he did not shoot Lamus.

The officer agreed, and grinning put his gun away. He and Schindler walked away arm in arm so that the officer could collect his bottle of schnapps from the stunned Oskar Schindler.

Lamus, he continued to walk across the courtyard, his pants around his ankles, waiting for a bullet from the officer or another to pierce his back. That bullet never came.

The frequency of incidents such as this continued to increase, which is probably why Schindler became more active in his antifascist role.

By the early spring of 1943, Schindler no longer worried about production, but instead, he focused on pulling strings, bribing, and conspiring the Nazi officials in order to save as many lives as he could.

It is at this point in his life that he becomes a true legend.

The Hero

During the 1944 and 1945, Schindler became obsessed with how he could save as many Jews as possible from Auschwitz, which was located just 60 kilometers from Krakow.

The first ambitious move that he made was to try and help those terrified prisoners of Plaszow that were starving. Plaszow seemed doomed at this point, the other camps that were located in Poland, such as Majdanek and Treblinka had already been liquidated.

However, Stern was able to convince Schindler to speak to one of his drinking buddies, a General Schindler, who was no relation to Oskar. However, this man was the chief of war-equipment command in Poland. Oskar was able to convince the

General that the workers that were located in Plaszow were perfect when it came to war-related production.

During this time, they were only repairing uniforms, however, the General agreed with Schindler and soon Plaszow was considered an essential camp for the war.

This did not help to improve the conditions, but it did remove the camp from the list of camps that were being liquidated. At least temporarily.

This also made Schindler look good in Amon Goeth's eyes because of this change, his status was elevated. It was then that Schindler requested a sub-camp for his workers in order 'to reduce the amount of time that it took them to get to work.'

Amon allowed for Schindler to have his own sub-camp and it was from that moment on that Schindler was able to have medicine and food brought in, to his workers without facing much danger.

Schindler, of course, bribed the guards that Amon had placed in the sub-camp ensuring that Amon would never learn of his true intentions for requesting the sub-camp.

Schindler soon began to take even bigger risks. At that time, it was very dangerous for anyone to intercede on behalf of a Jew, however, this was something that Schindler did on a regular basis.

He would usually tell them to stop killing his good workers, or that they had a war to win, they could settle their issues later.

This happened often enough that in doing so, Schindler was able to save more than a few dozen lives.

In August of 1943, two surprise visitors arrived from the American Jewish welfare agency which was an underground organization that operated in Europe.

Schindler urged Stern to speak with the men. They wanted a full report on the anti-Semitic persecution that the Jews were facing.

Oskar told Stern to speak frankly with the men, to let them know what had gone on in Plaszow. He told Stern that it was okay, to be honest with them, they were Swiss, he could trust them and to sit down and write a full report for them.

Stern was suspicious and became angry believing that it was a provocation. His anger and lack of trust sparked anger in Schindler, "Write," Schindler yelled at him, giving him no choice.

Stern sat and wrote down all that he could remember. He wrote down names of both the living and the dead, creating a long letter which only years later would he discover had been widely circulated. It would learn that his letter had helped settle the hearts of so many who were unable to find their relatives.

Once he received letters back from America, any doubts that may have still lingered on about Oskar Schindler disappeared.

Life continued on in Oskar Schindler's factory. Of course, there were those that died due to age or health issues, however, the majority of his workers continued working each day, creating enamelware. Schindler, however, wondered how long he would be able to continue with the game of deception that he had played for so long.

He still entertained the German officials, however, there had been a change in the tide and tempers were usually on edge. Oskar knew that with one stroke of the pen, any of his Jewish workers could have been sent to Auschwitz and he could have been sent as well.

He was cautious about his movements, increasing the bribes for the guards at his sub-camp, as well as the guards that had been placed in his factory. He used food and medicine to bribe the guards and fought for the survival of all of his Jews.

As 1944 began, each day, thousands of Polish Jews were killed, but all of Schindler's Jews were surprised to find that they were alive. By spring, the Germans were beginning to retreat and it was ordered that Plaszow, as well as all of the subcamps, be liquidated. Both Schindler and his workers knew what would happen if they were moved to another concentration camp and Schindler knew that it was time for him to put into play a plan that he had devised in case it would be needed.

Schindler, quickly sat out working on all of his drinking buddies, on all of the connections that he had within the military as well as the industrial circles in not only Krakow but Warsaw as well.

He persuaded, bribed, begged, and fought against time to ensure the safety of his Jews. He traveled to Berlin, and he refused to give up until he found someone that would allow him to remove his workforce of 700 men and 300 women from the camp and into his factory. That was exactly what he did.

The majority of the rest of the 25,000 prisoners that were kept in Plaszow were taken to Auschwitz, where they met the same fate as millions of other Jews who had already been sent there.

However, because of one crazy dedicated and stubborn man, 1000 sick, almost starved to death, broken humans were saved from a sentence of death.

Everyone was thrilled with the idea of leaving Poland and going to the new factory in Czechoslovakia, however, it would end up being one of the most terrifying events of their lives.

One group of 100 people did go straight to Brnenec, however, other workers found that their trains were diverted Gross-Rosen, a different concentration camp. When they arrived, they were beaten, tortured, and at one point, all of the prisoners were forced to stand in the courtyard in lines, continually putting their caps on and taking them off all day, in unison.

Schindler, however, would be successful at saving his Jews once again. He pulled strings and by November, his Jews arrived at their new camp.

It was also during this trip to their new factory in Brunnlitz that 300 of Schindler's female workers were taken to Auschwitz. Their lives were in danger as soon as they stepped off of the train.

However, this time, Schindler was unable to use his usual connections in order to rescue his workers. This time, he sent his secretary, Hilde Albrecht with food, diamonds and all types of black market items as bribes. After several weeks in Auschwitz, the women were finally sent to Brunnlitz.

In addition to his workers, Schindler had 250 wagon loads of raw material and machinery sent to his new factory, where artillery shells were going to be produced. There were very few shells that were ever produced at the plant and when questions began to arise about the low output, Schindler purchased shells that were already made on the black market and resold them.

The rations that the German officials provided was not enough to feed his workers so Schindler began spending most of his time in the procurement of food, as well as other items that his workers needed.

Emilie stayed in Brunnlitz at this time, doing what she could to provide health care to the workers, caring for them, providing health care, and meeting their basic needs.

It was also during this time that Oskar Schindler, arranged for 3,000 Jewish women who were in Auschwitz to be relocated to textile plants that were located in Sudetenland attempting to increase the chances that they survived the war.

In January of 1945, a train arrived in Brunnlitz with 250 Jews in it that had been rejected in Goleschau as mine workers. The doors had frozen shut and had to be opened with a soldering iron. There were 12 dead inside of the cars, many were too ill to work. It was Emilie, who took those that survived into the factory and provided care for them.

Jews who had escaped Auschwitz, as well as other camps, were taken in by Schindler. He had even requested that in the interest of continuing the war production that Gestapo sent all of the Jewish fugitives to him. He was able to save 100 more people by doing this.

Oskar was continuing to bribe the German officers in order to protect his workers. Then on May 8th, 1945, Oskar Schindler and his 'children' as he called them, gathered in his factory to listen to the radio as Winston Churchill announced that the war was over.

Oskar asked those that were in his factory to not go out and seek vengeance against those that had wronged them and he held a moment of silence for those that had lost their lives. To the SS officers that were present at the time, he asked that they peacefully return home and that no more bloodshed occur.

Schindler feared being captured because he had been part of the Nazi party. He also feared those that were in the Nazi party.

He continued to stay at his factory for a few days with about 1200 of his Jews, choosing to take his chances with the US forces that were approaching instead of being hunted down by the Germans. However, it was a single Russian officer, who freed Schindler and his Jews after riding up to Schindler's factory on a horse.

There were 801 men and 287 women that Schindler called his children.

Oskar understood the fears of those that he cared for and took care of. When he moved them to the new factory, he was given a villa that overlooked the factory, however, because his 'children' feared the SS officials might come in the middle of the night and kill them, Oskar and Emilie instead, slept in one of the rooms in the factory, never spending a single night at the villa.

When one of his Jewish workers died, he allowed the others to bury the worker with full rites, even though the Nazi's had ruled that the bodies were to be burned. He allowed his workers to observe their religious holidays.

After the War

After the end of the war, Schindler's life was not much different than it had been before. He tried many things and only saw failure, once he even tried to become a film producer but once again he failed.

Schindler's nationality was even taken from him after the war ended. He was threatened by former Nazi party members, which made him fear for his and his wife's safety. Therefore, he tried to gain entry into the US, however, he was refused because he had joined the Nazi party.

After being denied entry into the US, Oskar and Emilia went to Buenos Aires, Argentina along with about a dozen of his Jews and his mistress.

In 194, Schindler had settled down and lived on a farm. During this time, the Jewish Organization Joint, as well as other thankful Jews, supported him.

However, Oskar would not find success and in 1957 he was bankrupt. He left Argentina and Emilie to return to Europe. It was the last time that he would see his wife.

Oskar found himself an apartment that was located at Am Hauptbahn Nr. 4 which was in Frankfurt, Germany. This time, he tried to find success without the help from any Jewish organizations. He wanted to run a cement factory. However, in 1961 Schindler was bankrupt once again.

Then in 1962, Oskar was honored in Israel, named a Righteous Gentile. This honor caused his German partner to cancel their partnership. The partner told Schindler that it was clear that he was a friend to the Jews and that the two would no longer work together.

At this point in his life, Schindler was completely dependent upon the Jews that he had saved, relying on their gifts and money to support him. Poldek Pfefferberg encouraged each of Schindler's Jews to donate one day's pay to him each year in order to help support him.

Moshe Beijske, who was another of Schindler's Jews, who had become the Israeli High Court Judge, lovingly stated that if you sent Oskar 3 thousand dollars, he would be broke in a matter of a few weeks, calling to say that he did not have a cent left.

On top of all of the hatred that was directed at Oskar Schindler after the war by the Germans, it was only fed by his involvement in the trials of Nazi war criminals. Oskar was sworn at while he was on the streets of Germany, he had rocks thrown at him, and he faced continual persecution.

It is said that Oskar Schindler was a reminder to them. He was a reminder to all that had done nothing, to all who had believed the propaganda, a reminder that they could have saved lives.

At one point, a worker in his cement factory called Schindler a Jew Kisser. Schindler reacted by boxing the man's ears, which lead to Schindler being taken to court for the violence. It was in court that the judge lectured Schindler on the law.

At one point Schindler wrote a letter to one of the Jews that he saved, telling them that had it not have given the Germans so much satisfaction, he would have taken his own life.

Oskar has been honored all across the world by Jews and Gentiles alike. He was an unlikely hero, one that saw the humanity in the Jews that were being slaughtered by the thousands every day.

He died on October 9, 1974, of liver failure in Germany. He was laid to rest in the Mount Zion Catholic Cemetery in Jerusalem. The place where he had requested to be buried because that was where his children were.

Why

So many have found themselves over the years asking why. Why did Oskar Schindler risk everything to save the lives of Jews? Why did Oskar Schindler go against the Nazi party of which he belonged to? Why did he take all of the money that he had earned and spent it on those workers? Why would he take his one chance at success and waste it?

Oskar Schindler never gave any clear answer as to why he did what he did. He never told anyone why he felt compelled to save the lives of the Jews that he saved. Some believe that his actions should not need any explanation, that Oskar acted as a human to other humans but did he?

When we look back at the time of World War II, you have to understand that Oskar could have easily gone along with the Nazi party. He could have used the Jews for their labor, he could have profited greatly from the war, and no one would have threatened his life, taken from him, or thrown rocks at him when it was all over.

In fact, Oskar Schindler could have done nothing to save a single Jew, he could have run his business, taken his money, and let whatever was going to happen to them happen.

Once, Oskar described his behaviors during the war, stating that he had no other choice. He said that if a person saw a dog that was getting ready to be crushed under a car, they would help. He felt that he had done what he had to do.

However, Schindler's Jews had their own explanations for his actions.

Johnathan Dresner said that Schindler was an adventurer. Schindler was like an actor in that he always wanted to be on the center of the stage. Once he got into the play, he found that he had no way to get out of it.

According to Mosche Bejski, Oskar was a womanizer and a drunkard. He had a bad relationship with his wife and not only had one girlfriend but several. However, everything that he did to protect his Jews, put his life in jeopardy. Oskar Schindler did what no normal man would have been able to.

Danka Dresner stated that the Jews, he saved owed their lives to him, however, she would not glorify a German because of what he did for them.

Abraham Zuckerman stated about the Schindler's List movie, that it did not show the little things that Oskar did for the Jews that worked in his factory. Oskar would go around, greet the workers. He stated that because of Oskar, he had protection, food, and hope.

Salomon Pila said that he did not know why Oskar Schindler was so good to them, but that he would tell Oskar thank you because it was Oskar that saved his life.

One of the women that was rescued from Auschwitz, Helen Beck, said that she would never forget seeing Oskar Schindler when she arrived at Brunnlitz. He told her not to worry that she was with him now. She recalled that the group gave up many times, however, Schindler was always there to lift their spirits. He did what he could to help people.

Ludwik Feigenbaum said that he did not know what Schindler's motives were. He said that when he did ask him, he did not receive a clear answer. Referring to the movie, Schindler's List, he stated that it was not made clear there either. However, he stated that he didn't care what the motive was, all that was important was that Oskar saved their lives.

Ludwik made a great point. While so many find themselves wondering why Oskar did what he did, we have to remind ourselves that his motives do not matter. What does it matter with the lives of all of the Jewish people that he saved?

Schindler's List

The movie, Schindler's List is moving, touching, heartbreaking, and amazing, but we have to ask ourselves one question. Is the movie accurate?

The first thing that we have to remember is that the movie is just that. It is a movie and not a documentary. The movie is based on a true story and it does contain some of the accounts of those that were in Krakow, however, it is not a retelling of the actual events that happened.

The truth is that the movie is based off of Schindler's Ark, which is a historical fiction book by Thomas Keneally.

The book was released in the US under the name of Schindler's List in 1982 and then was later adapted into the movie.

In 1983, the book was awarded the Los Angeles Time Book Prize. In the book, you find the historical fiction story of Oskar Schindler. A historical fiction book means that while the book does describe actual people, places, and events, there are also fictional events and dialogue added when the exact details of what occurred is not known.

It was Poldek Pfeffferberg, one of Oskar's Jews that we have spoken about on several occasions that inspired the author to write the book. Poldek had many times after the end of the war tried to get many different screenwriters and well as filmmakers interested in the story of Schindler. He told them the story of how Oskar had saved the Polish Jews from sure death and even arranged television interviews in the United States for Oskar.

Poldek had immigrated to the US after the war and in 1980 he owned a shop in Beverly Hills. It is there that he met Keneally when the author came into the shop and asked for the prices of briefcases.

At this time, Keneally had been at a book signing in Beverly Hills and was returning home to Australia. After Poldek learned that Keneally was an author, he showed them the files which he kept in the back of the store on Oskar Schindler.

It took a total of 50 minutes before Keneally agreed to write a book about Oskar. Poldek accompanied Keneally to Poland, where the two visited Krakow as well as other areas that were associated with Oskar.

When the book was finally published, it was dedicated to Poldeck Pfefferberg.

After the book was published, Steven Spielberg was persuaded by Poldeck to make the film.

What makes Keneally's version different is that it focuses on the fact that Oskar Schindler was a flawed man, that while he was a hero, he was by no means perfect.

In one interview, Emilie stated that Oskar Schindler had done nothing remarkable neither before nor after the war, but that in the years between 1939 and 1945 he had met a group of people that forced him to use his true talents.

Knowing this, we can determine that Schindler's list was based on true events.

Many of the critics of the movie have pointed out that it can not be seen as something that represents what happened during the Holocaust. This is a very true statement. The story is that what one man accomplished during the war. It is a story of 1200 lives that were saved and about the events that happened in one single concentration camp.

The Holocaust could never be represented in just one movie. Millions of lives were destroyed, families were ripped apart.

There are also things in the movie as well as in the book that are used as symbols because the fact is that there was no accurate information passed on. On top of this, we have to remember that it was just a movie. There were things added in, edited out and created to increase the dramatic effect.

One example of this would be the little girl walking through the streets in the red coat. This little girl can reach deep into the mind and soul, pulling at every human emotion, but in reality, she was never there.

What about the fact that Schindler was sleeping with the enemy throughout the entire movie. The way that he interacted with Amon Goeth, the words that came out of his mouth as he agreed with the Nazi's. Of course, we do not know exactly what was said, we can only speculate, but we have to remember that going into the enamelware business, he had no intention of saving anyone.

Oskar Schindler joined the Nazi party to ensure that Oskar Schindler benefited. He opened the enamelware factory in order to become rich. It would not be surprising to find that he was being friendly with the Nazi party. Even as he was risking his life to save those whose life hung in the balance every minute of every day, it is no wonder that he tried to stay in the good graces of the Nazi party.

Another problem that many have with the book, as well as the movie, is that Oskar is depicted as someone who might be a bit carefree and a playboy, however, he was a bit worse than that.

In one of the scenes of the movie, Amon looks at Schindler as they stand on the balcony after Helena refills their drinks. Amon falls to the floor and crawls into a seat. He tells Oskar that he has watched him and that he is never drunk. "That is power," he tells Oskar.

While we already understand that the majority of the dialogue in the movie is made up, we can be sure that this never took place. Schindler was an alcoholic who died from liver poisoning. We can therefore almost be sure that he was drunk more than once.

However, authors have to create a hero that they know the audience will like and because this was not a documentary, they were able to do so.

The little girl in red was never watched by Schindler as he sat atop his horse watching as the Nazi's slaughtered people. Instead, Keneally was told about a little girl who used to like to wear a red cap. She was rounded up in 1942 and taken to a place that was close to the Optima Factory. She was never in Plaszow. Which means that it would have been impossible for Schindler to ever see the girl.

In reality, Schindler was atop the hill in March of 1943 so it is much more likely that the little girl was added into the story. His mistress, was with him on the hilltop, in the movie, she is called Ingrid however, his mistresses names, in reality, were Marta and

Eva. Of course, it is entirely possible that Schindler had other mistresses.

One of the very powerful scenes in the movie is when the women are taken to Auschwitz. After having their heads shaved they are herded into what they believe to be gas chambers.

However, according to those that were there at the time, they had no idea that the Nazi's had used gassing as their preferred method of killing. There was no way that the women would have expected to be gassed, but instead, they would have expected that they would have been showered.

In the movie, we can see the fear and the panic as the water begins pouring out of the shower heads, however, this did not happen. The women had just arrived at Auschwitz, and they did not know about the mass deaths that were taking place in concentration camps. Nor did they know that the gas chambers were disguised as showers.

According to one of the women that was there, none of the women knew anything of gas chambers when they arrived at Auschwitz. They had gone through the initial selection and had survived. And while they did know that being a Polish Jew lowered their chances of ever getting to leave Auschwitz, they had never heard of the victims being led to showers to be 'disinfected' as is depicted in the movie.

After the initial selection, the women had their heads shaved and were taken to the showers. The water was briefly turned on before they were given filthy uniforms that they were to wear while there.

Of course, trying to depict the horror that is felt being in Auschwitz or any other concentration camp is utterly impossible and this scene was added so that the viewer could understand just a bit of what the people went through upon their arrival, the fear that they felt.

The movie also gives the impression that Oskar Schindler wrote the list, adding more and more names to it frantically until the very end. However, history shows that Schindler really did not have a lot to do with the list.

History shows us that there were nine lists. Marcel Goldberg drew up four of the lists.

Marcel Goldberg, who is described as a corrupt Jew who served as a police officer as well as an assistant to the SS officer that was in charge of the transportation of Jews. (Later, Goldberg was accused of favoritism as well as accepting bribes.)

While Schindler did suggest that a few names be added to the list, he did not know the majority of those that were on the list. No one knows who the author of the five remaining lists was.

It is claimed that Schindler used the 'list' to embellish when it came to his own heroism. He was supposedly supposed to be trying to acquire reparations for all of the money that he lost during the war. He did receive around 13,000 dollars, however, his losses were in the millions.

It is also said that the character of Amon Goeth in the movie had to be toned down quite a bit. It is said that if all of Goeth's actions had been put into the film his character would not have been far too evil and simply unbelievable.

He was known for murdering people daily, trained his dogs to kill those in the camp at command. He beat the maids that he had in his house, he would have the entire work detail killed if a single person had escaped and as depicted in the movie, he did shoot people from his balcony.

He was a cowardly disgusting man who took pleasure in killing the women and the children during the liquidation of the ghettos. The person that was depicted in the film is far from the man that he truly was.

While the film is wonderful, moving, and it guarantees that no one will ever forget what the Jewish people went through during WWII, it is a work of fiction, one that is based on actual events but not a true depiction of what occurred.

If it were a true depiction of the events, the conversations, and the men that were in charge of Krakow, it would not have been as big of a hit as it was.

Yes, Oskar Schindler would have still been known as a hero, but the torture, horror, and complete hell that the people experienced is not something that anyone would find 'entertaining.'

The Suitcase

It was in October of 1999 when a suitcase was found that belonged to Oskar Schindler. The suitcase was filled with papers, including the list of his Jewish employees that were saved from death at the hands of the Nazi's.

The suitcase had been left to a couple whose children later gave it to Stuttgarter Zeitung, who was a reporter for a German newspaper, who said that he had planned on giving the suitcase to Yad Vashem.

It was a gray suitcase, old and worn with a tag on it that read, 'O. Schindler.'

The suitcase was found by a couple who had been cleaning out the home of their parents which had recently passed. The parents had been close friends of Oskar Schindler, who had lived near him in Frankfurt.

It was in this suitcase that the couple found the list of the workers among many other papers which mostly dealt with Oskar's life after the war

There were writings about how the German citizens treated him, how he struggled with alcohol, his affairs, the connections that he had in Israel, as well as the Jews that were still in Germany.

There were letters that had been exchanged between the 40's and 60's as well as a speech that he had written that he gave to the Jews on his factory floor at the end of the war. It was this speech in which he requested that the Jews search for their families and not become violent searching for revenge against those that had done so much harm.

The list that was found was on a paper with the letterhead from the Enamelware Factory which was located in Krakow. On it was the name of 1200 Jews that were located in the Plaszow concentration camp.

It was the same list that had been given to the Nazi SS on it, it stated that those people were needed in the factory.

Fictitious jobs had been added to the list for each of the workers whose name was on it to ensure that the Nazi's were convinced that they were essential to the war effort which would ensure that they were allowed to live.

It is believed that Schindler kept one copy and that another copy was kept in the SS archives.

Michel Friedman, a descendant of two of Schindler's Jews felt that the papers in the suitcase were very important because they confirmed that after WWII Oskar's economic situation was extremely bad. It also showed that the only people that helped him were the Jews. Not the German government who was in charge of paying the pensions to the Nazis.

He stated that Oskar had been the guest of honor at his bar Mitzvah and that he came to their home for Sabbath dinners. Which showed, that Oskar did what he could to remain in contact with his Jews.

In the suitcase, there is also a message for the Germans that is quite unpleasant. The letters in the suitcase showed how a man who the Germans knew had rescued Jews ended up being rejected and isolated even after the war ended by his fellow Germans.

Looking back today, Oskar Schindler is not just a great example to Germans but to the entire world, however, at the time, people did not want to know about him nor his story.

At that time, many German's claimed that they had no idea what was going on in the concentration camps, however, looking back at the publications in the newspapers it is impossible to believe this.

It is more likely that they did not want to accept what was happening. Seeing

Schindler and hearing his story reminded them of what they had tried to ignore, what they had tried to forget was happening. It reminded them that they, one single person, could have done something.

In the letters Oskar Schindler talks about how Germany was not interested in seeing what had happened during the war, they did not want to admit that there was a Holocaust. It upset Schindler quite a bit that they were not interested in that part of their history, that they wanted to hear nothing of it.

Instead of wanting to understand what had happened, and ensure that it never happened again, they chose to be angry with Schindler for making a good impression on the nation of Israel.

The suitcase was old, it had been taken on many trips. When it was opened, there were many old papers and old letters. All of it completely disorganized.

The papers in the suitcase allow the reader to understand what it was like to be a prisoner, he was an open-minded man and spoke freely, he wrote what he was thinking and in the letters, you are able to see that he had a lot of hope but he also faced a lot of disappointment as well.

Those that found the suitcase stated that upon first impression they were unsure what to do with the suitcase because there were so many pictures, letters, and newspaper articles in it. They sat around each evening reading the contents trying to figure out how to publish it, but not wanting to move too quickly.

In fact, they actually kept the finding of the suitcase a secret for nearly a year. The journalist who obtained the suitcase was going to write a biography using the material that was in the suitcase however, he decided against it.

He did, however, choose to create a series that was titled, "Schindler's Suitcase," which he began running on the 25th anniversary of the death of Schindler.

According to the experts that Yad Vashem, the list is likely not the original, however, the papers that are contained in the suitcase allow us to see into the complicated life of Oskar Schindler.

There is the man who wants to be the man that he was during WWII. He was the owner of a large company, however, after the war, it simply was not possible.

The letters allow the reader to really get to know someone that they had never met. To feel as if they have an intimate relationship with him.

It was in 2015 that due to the suitcase and the contents in it, Yad Vashem Holocaust Memorial found itself in the middle of a legal case with Emilie Schindler to determine who actually owned the list.

On April 15th, 2015, a preliminary case was held in order to decide if the list was the property of Vad Vashem Holocaust Memorial or if it would go to Erika Rosenburg who was not only the beneficiary but also the executor of Emilie Schindler's estate.

The list that was in question contained the names of 801 of the Jews that had worked in Schindler's factory, which he had protected from the Nazi's during WWII.

Yad Vashem is a memorial to the Holocaust, focusing on ensuring that the events are never forgotten and that they never happen again.

It was in 1999 that the memorial received the suitcase that contained thousands of documents which included two of the remaining copies of the list, which there are only four left in existence. Originally there had been seven copies that had been typed out on onionskin paper.

The suitcase, as well as the immeasurable valuable contents, had been left by Schindler with Anne-Marie Staehr who was one of Schindler's mistresses before it was found and presented to the press. It was finally sent to Yad Vashem by Ulrich Sahm, who was a German journalist as well as a resident of Jerusalem.

Both parties agreed that this was how the suitcase and the papers ended up at Yad Vashem, however, what they disagree on is who has the rightful claim to the contents of the suitcase.

Rosenberg claimed that Staehr stole the documents from Schindler's home after he died and kept them hidden in the suitcase until he died in 1984. The suitcase was forgotten about until it was found 15 years later by his son.

Emilie learned of the document's existence by reading the newspaper stories about her deceased husband and asked Rosenberg to retrieve them for her.

However, when she went to Stuttgarter Zeitung and demanded that they give the documents to her, she was informed that Yad Vashem in Jerusalem already had possession of them.

Rosenburg told the Haaretz, which is a daily newspaper in Israel, that Emilie had become ill because of the affair. Emilie had stated that it as 'a huge injustice.'

According to Rosenburg, Emilie had told her that she had saved Jews along with her husband and now it was the Jews that had taken the suitcase from her. She told Rosenburg that she had to demand it be returned, even after her death.

Emilie had returned to Germany in 2001 where she died, leaving no descendants. Rosenburg filed a lawsuit against Yad Vashem in 2013, accusing them of theft.

Rosenburg's attorney stated that even if the documents should remain at Yad Vashem due to their historical value, they had no right to take what belonged to someone else.

According to Yad Vashem, the documents were obtained legally and they have been transparent about how they were obtained.

The memorial stated that Schindler had given the suitcase to Staehr on his own and that because he had voluntarily done this, it had never belonged to Emilie in the first place.

The memorial stated that because of their historical value the documents needed to remain public domain.

In February of 2015, Yad Vashem requested that the charges be dismissed, however, they were denied that request by the Jerusalem District Court.

Yad Vashem feared that the documents would reach private hands of someone who was only interested in making money off of something that did not belong to them.

Rosenburg however, always claimed that she only wanted to protect and preserve the documents. However, in July of 2013, one of the copies of one of Schindler's lists was sold on eBay for around three million dollars.

Rosenburg had also tried and failed to stop the sale of the list claiming that it infringed upon copyright laws. She stated that because Emilie had left her estate to her, the list was not to be published.

Again she stated that she had no interest in profiting from the list, but instead wanted to protect, preserve, as well as correct the record.

Emilie Schindler's Last Days

In her last days, Emilie Schindler was angry. She was angry at Steven Spielberg, claiming that he had only given her 50 thousand dollars for making the film Schindler's List and that he had never asked her permission to do so.

She demanded that she receive 6 percent of the proceeds that were made off of the movie stating that Spielberg knew nothing of her life.

She not only lashed out at Spielberg, but at other's as well. She began by stating that there was never a 'Schindler's List' that in fact it had been written by Goldman.

She stated that Goldman had taken money to put names on the list that if there was no money, the name was not put on the list.

She was also angry that her husband was thought of as a hero. She had stated that she saved thousands of Jews as well, insisting that it was she that has signed documents which had saved the Jews from almost certain death that they would face in Auschwitz.

It was obvious that she was still the jilted wife that he had left long before. She said that she was an idiot for falling in love with Schindler, but that she would never cry over him, there was no sense in doing so.

According to Emilie, Oskar changed women as often as he changes suits. She had admitted that at one point in their lives they were well off, but that he had lost everything and then abandoned her. She admitted that she never recovered.

She even stated that neither of them were heroes. She said that Oskar was a complex man, but even to the end he was playing both sides, the Jews against the Nazi's and the Nazi's against the Jews.

The words of an angry wife that had been cheated on numerous times? Or the truth from the woman that was there?

Oskar was never going to win the husband of the year award, however, as many would agree, there is no reason to try and take away from the fact that he saved thousands of lives, no matter what his motives were.

Lessons From Oskar Schindler

Each year all across the world, people learn the story of Oskar Schindler for the first time or the revisit it in order to learn lessons they may have overlooked.

People look to the story of Oskar Schindler for hope that somewhere out there in the world, there are still people who care, but what can we learn in our world today from Oskar Schindler?

It is an easy thing to go about our lives and not think about the things that have happened in the past, the things that continue to happen every day in our world.

It is very easy for us to block out the horrors of the events of the past when we get to focus on the next season of our favorite show coming out on Netflix.

However, those horrors, they will always be there, they are never going to disappear from our history and that is why Schindler's story is so important. In fact, that is why even as historical fiction, Schindler's list is one of the most important movies that has ever been made.

There are those of us that find ourselves thinking about the events of the Holocaust on a daily basis. We look at our children and wonder how we would face the horrors that the Jewish people faced.

How would we handle being separated from our children? How would we react if they were loaded into trucks and taken to a death camp? Could we be as strong as those that came before us and continue to go on? Could we in the face of hell on Earth, continue to find a reason to live?

The murder of 6 million Jews is the most devastating crime to have been committed in the history of this world. To spend one day not recognizing those events is disgraceful.

What do we need to learn? The first thing that we have to understand as we look through history is that it tends to repeat itself. Especially if it is not learned from.

We can, however, ensure that history does not repeat itself and that no more Oskar Schindler's are ever needed in this world.

The story of Oskar Schindler is not only a story of unbelievable tragedy, but it is also one of love, joy, life, and hope.

As dire as the events of the Holocaust were, Oskar Schindler was able to save over a thousand lives. Simply thinking about that number is mind boggling. One thousand lives that would have been lost had it not been for the actions of one member of the Nazi party.

The idea that one man could accomplish so much is staggering. One man did so much good in this world.

His story is hope because it is education. We do not need to feel despair because while the events that took place are horrid, by educating ourselves, we can ensure that it never happens to anyone ever again.

That is the most important thing that we can do in the world that we live in today. You see, once an event occurs, we are able to recognize the events that led up to it in the past which enables us to recognize those same events today. This enables us to ensure no one suffers in this way again.

What can we learn from Oskar Schindler as a man? He was not an exceptional man. He had failed at everything he attempted in his life. He had affairs, was an alcoholic, was broke and yet in the face of adversity, he was able to overcome all of his failures and to become one of the most beloved and heroic men to live.

Not only did he save the lives of 1200 Jews, he saved a nation. He saved what became over 15,000 Jewish lives as of 2017. He saved a nation that was threatened to be wiped off of the map. One that is still threatened to this day to be wiped off of the map.

He did not let his failures hold him back from doing what he knew was right. When he was faced with true evil, he did not listen to what he was being told about the Jewish people.

Instead, he listened to what his heart told him. He saw that even though the propaganda that was being pushed at him claimed that the Jews were not people, that they were not human, in fact, they were human, just like him.

Schindler saw that they bled the same blood, he did, even if they were Jews. He saw that their lives were important and he refused to let evil prevail.

Oskar Schindler allows us to learn important lessons from WWII, which was the deadliest conflict in the history of the world.

It was WWII that changed the course of the world, but have we really learned the important lessons?

During WWII, there was a clear definition between good and evil. Had true evil won, chances are that you would not be reading this book in English, in fact, you would not be reading this book at all because as he said, "Today, we rewrite history."

It as Hitler's intention to wipe any record of the Jewish people from history. If evil had won, our world would be a different place.

But good won. The Schindler's of the world, hid in the midst of all evil, protecting innocent people.

However, as the generation that lived and fought in the war disappears, the war is being forgotten. The world is choosing to allow amnesia to take over their minds. Which is why the world that we are living in has some of the problems that it does today.

It began with the reduction of personal liberties. The government, telling people what they needed and did not need. It started with the disarming of the citizens, ensuring that it was only the SS that had the weapons.

Hitler wrote, "The most foolish mistake that we could make is to allow the Jews to possess arms."

People vote, allowing their liberties to be taken away, not realizing that they are doing the same thing that once led to gas chambers, ovens, and concentration camps. Yet we hear, "Never forget," on a regular basis.

From the ashes, of this conflict, what did we learn? Did we learn that all people deserve a nation of their own? Did we learn that all people are created equal and equally deserve the right to live?

Did we learn that in a crisis, it does not matter what your religion, race, or skin color? Or that we need to stand up for each other even when we are different?

No.

Today, there are many who refused to accept that the state of Israel actually deserves to exist. There are still those that want to wipe the Jewish people from the planet. Sadly, there are still those that follow the teachings of Adolf Hitler, committing heinous crimes in his name.

If we have not learned our lesson from WWII what is it going to take for us to learn it?

The slaughter of millions of people happened just around 70 years ago. Many of those that suffered in those camps, many of those that lost their parents, and many of those that fought in that war are still alive today.

We can look at their faces, and we can hear their stories. We see men and women who like Oskar Schindler risked everything in order to help keep people that meant nothing to them safe from the murderous hands of the Nazis.

What happens when those faces are gone and they are no longer there to remind us of what once happened?

Are we doomed to repeat history? Sadly, the answer is yes and we are standing on the brink of it as you read this. We are living in an era where once again, the Jewish people are attacked for doing nothing more than existing.

Anti-Semitism Today

Anti-Semitism, a hostility that is directed against the Jewish people. It exists no matter how much people want to sweep it under the rug.

It has existed since the beginning of the Jewish people. Even since the end of the Holocaust, the Jewish people continue to endure hatred for no other reason than that they are Jews.

Today, there is a new strain of Anti-Semitism that is more political and focused on the State of Israel than it is to the actual Jewish people.

The driving factor is the Palestinian/Israeli conflict.

In 1948 Israel was declared a state and soon the quarrel of who the land actually belonged to began.

Today, the Jewish people face blasts, rockets, stones being thrown over the wall at their children and so much more every single day.

Anti-Semitism has lingered in the US, Europe, and all across the globe, even though it has been years since the war ended.

The new Anti-Semitism while based off of political reasons more than religious or racial is still as dangerous as the old Anti-Semitism because the annualization of the Jews is still being called for.

I cannot help but ask myself, what would Oskar Schindler think of this world that we are living in? Of the world that seems to want all of his 'children', their children, and their grandchildren dead?

What would he say to those that do not believe that the Jewish people deserve a little country that is no more than three miles wide?

I fear that his heart would be broken and that he would feel once again as a failure.

A man who was part of the Nazi party, who had no more interest in the war than to make a profit, gave everything that he had, risked his life and died feeling like nothing more than a failure so that 15,000 descendants of his Jews could live today.

In the last chapter, I talked about the lessons that we could learn from Oskar Schindler.

There is one lesson that I think the world needs more than any other today.

It is that it does not matter what color your skin, what your religion or your race, it does not matter if you agree or disagree, if you are friends or if you are completely opposite from each other. A life is still a life and when you save just one life, you can save the entire world.

There was one scene in the movie Schindler's List that I will never forget. It has always stuck with me and it is one that Stern himself stated was an actual event.

At the end of the movie, Oskar began to cry, realizing that he could have done so much more. "This car," he says, "I could have sold this car." He grabs his pin, "Two lives," he continues, "I could have saved two more, one at least one."

At the end of the war, this man who had done so much, who had saved so many people, felt that he had not done enough. He saw all of the ways that he could have saved more lives.

I don't know if he ever realized what a difference he made in the world, or if in some life beyond this one, he was shown, but Oskar Schindler did not only affect the lives of 1200 Jews that he saved in his factory.

Oskar Schindler affected the lives of 15,000 Jews that are alive today because of him. He has affected the lives of almost everyone that has ever learned about his life. He will continue to affect lives for years to come.

He will give people hope, that they are not alone in the world. He will remind them that when they see someone in need, to help them because they have no other choice but to do what is right

He will remind us that no matter how many times we have failed in the past, no matter how many times we have tried and found ourselves at the lowest point we think we can reach, deep within us is the strength to make a difference when it is needed.

Oskar Schindler has shown us that one person just one person doing what he or she knows is the right thing, can actually change the entire world.

We must continue to share the stories of the Holocaust with the generations to come. We need to make sure that they learn from the mistakes of those that came before us so that they never have to face a situation like that, but we also need to continue to remind them that in the face of the worst evil that has ever walked on this earth there were men like Oskar Schindler.

Men and women out there standing strong, putting their lives on the line for people that they were supposed to hate. Risking everything for people that they did not know simply because they knew that it was the right thing to do.

Yes, Oskar Schindler was a failure. He was a cheat, boisterous, arrogant, a womanizer, a man that most people would never look at as a hero today and yet, he was able to overcome everything that stood in his way to save his Jews.

If Oskar Schindler, just one man could in the face of all of that adversity save the lives of 1200 humans, there is nothing that we cannot do. There is no reason that we cannot help those around us, no matter how we feel about them.

If Oskar Schindler, could touch the lives of so many people, we can with even the smallest acts of kindness, touch the lives of a few. We don't have to aspire to be Oskar Schindler and save the world, it takes a special type of person to do what he did, but we can each day, do what we can to make a difference in someone's life.

To those 1200 Jews, this failure at business, this man who was a member of the Nazi party, was their protector, the one thing that was standing between them and the Nazis that wished to see them dead.

Filled with flaws, he was the most unlikely of heroes, but he is a man that we can all look up to, one that continues to save the faith that we have in humanity.

Printed in Poland
by Amazon Fulfillment
Poland Sp. z o.o., Wrocław